Blue Bonds for Ocean Sustainability: A Global Climate Solutions Insight on Sustainable Finance, Water Security, and Marine Resilience

Copyright

Blue Bonds for Ocean Sustainability: A Global Climate Solutions Insight on Sustainable Finance, Water Security, and Marine Resilience

ISBN 978-1-991369-49-9 (eBook)

ISBN 978-1-991369-50-5 (Paperback)

Cover design by Global Climate Solutions

First edition, 2025

Table of Contents

Executive Summary

Blue bonds are an emerging financial instrument designed to mobilize capital for the sustainable management and protection of marine and coastal ecosystems. As ocean health faces increasing pressures from climate change, pollution, and unsustainable resource use, blue bonds offer a targeted mechanism to finance activities that support biodiversity, coastal resilience, and ocean-based economic development. By directing funds to ocean-related projects, blue bonds help align financial markets with global sustainability goals, including the Sustainable Development Goals (particularly SDG 14), the Paris Agreement, and the Kunming-Montreal Global Biodiversity Framework.

This Insight outlines the foundational conditions needed to expand the blue bond market with integrity and scale. Chapter 1 focuses on the policy and governance frameworks required to establish market credibility, including regulatory standards, legal structures, and institutional coordination. Chapter 2 examines financing structures and market development strategies, highlighting the role of blended finance, investor alignment, and project pipeline creation. Chapter 3 explores the importance of digital systems, ocean data infrastructure, and impact measurement tools in promoting transparency and accountability.

Together, these chapters present a strategic pathway for governments, development institutions, and private sector actors to advance blue bond adoption. Key recommendations include integrating blue finance into national policy frameworks, building institutional capacity, enhancing investor engagement through risk mitigation, and investing in digital tools that enable robust monitoring and reporting.

Scaling the blue bond market is both a challenge and an opportunity. With the right policy, financial, and technological foundations, blue bonds can become a core instrument in financing a sustainable, resilient, and inclusive ocean economy.

Introduction

Blue bonds have emerged as a targeted financial instrument designed to address the growing need for sustainable investment in marine and coastal ecosystems. As climate change, pollution, and overexploitation continue to degrade ocean health, there is increasing recognition of the ocean's role in climate regulation, biodiversity, food security, and economic stability. In this context, blue bonds offer a mechanism to mobilize capital toward the protection and sustainable use of ocean resources, aligning financial flows with global sustainability objectives.

While conceptually similar to green and sustainability bonds, blue bonds are distinct in their exclusive focus on ocean-related projects. These may include marine conservation, pollution reduction, coastal resilience, and sustainable fisheries. The bond structure remains familiar to investors, but the use of proceeds is directed solely toward initiatives that support ocean health and resilience. This specificity allows for enhanced transparency and impact alignment, but also requires clearer definitions, frameworks, and verification processes to build investor confidence and market credibility.

This Insight provides a high-level, solutions-focused overview for global sustainability professionals and decision-makers. It is structured into three chapters, each addressing one critical dimension: enabling policy frameworks, financial mechanisms and market development, and the role of technology and data systems in strengthening transparency and accountability across the blue bond ecosystem.

Chapter 1: Policy and Governance Frameworks for Blue Bond Credibility

The successful development of the blue bond market depends on the establishment of strong policy and governance frameworks. As a relatively new financing instrument, blue bonds require clear regulatory direction, credible institutional oversight, and alignment with broader sustainability goals to gain the confidence of issuers, investors, and stakeholders.

Public policy defines the strategic scope of blue bonds by integrating them into national ocean plans, climate commitments, and sustainable development agendas. At the same time, governance mechanisms ensure that proceeds are used responsibly and transparently, with appropriate safeguards and reporting standards in place.

This chapter outlines the foundational elements required to support a credible blue bond market. It explores the role of enabling policy, regulatory standards, institutional arrangements, and verification systems, and discusses how coherence across sectors and targeted risk reduction strategies can further strengthen the enabling environment for sustainable ocean finance.

1.1 The Role of Policy in Shaping the Blue Bond Market

Public policy plays a foundational role in establishing the conditions necessary for a credible and functional blue bond market. As demand grows for financial instruments that align with environmental objectives, national and regional policies must provide the regulatory clarity and strategic direction needed to guide blue bond development and ensure alignment with broader sustainability agendas.

Blue bonds function most effectively when integrated within national ocean governance frameworks, climate action plans, and sustainable development strategies. Governments can strengthen investor confidence and project eligibility by embedding blue finance within long-term policy commitments, including Nationally Determined Contributions (NDCs), marine spatial planning, and coastal resilience initiatives. Such alignment helps establish blue bonds not as isolated instruments, but as tools contributing to defined policy outcomes.

Policy also plays a critical role in coordinating across ministries and sectors. Blue bond projects often span multiple domains—such as fisheries, energy, tourism, and infrastructure—requiring cohesive governance and cross-institutional collaboration. Policymakers can facilitate this by establishing inter-ministerial working groups or designated blue finance coordination units.

At the regional and international levels, policy can promote harmonization of standards, reduce fragmentation, and support knowledge exchange. Aligning national approaches with global frameworks—such as the Sustainable Development Goals (particularly SDG 14), the Paris Agreement, and the Kunming-Montreal Global Biodiversity Framework—reinforces the legitimacy of blue bonds and broadens their appeal to global investors. Ultimately, sound public policy enables a stable foundation for the issuance, credibility, and long-term integration of blue bonds into sustainable finance systems.

1.2 Regulatory Standards and Classification

Clear regulatory standards and classification systems are essential to the development of a transparent and credible blue bond market. Without agreed definitions or eligibility criteria, there is a risk of inconsistent application, reduced investor confidence, and potential misuse of proceeds. Regulatory frameworks help ensure that blue bonds deliver measurable environmental outcomes, particularly in areas related to marine conservation, sustainable resource use, and ocean resilience.

Currently, blue bonds often draw from existing green or sustainability bond principles, such as the International Capital Market Association's (ICMA) Green Bond Principles and the Sustainability-Linked Bond Principles. While these frameworks provide useful guidance, they are not tailored to the unique characteristics of marine and coastal investments. As such, there is growing interest in developing dedicated blue bond taxonomies that outline acceptable project types, reporting expectations, and environmental safeguards specific to ocean-related activities.

A consistent classification system would help standardize the types of projects eligible for financing, such as coral reef restoration, marine protected area expansion, sustainable aquaculture, or wastewater reduction. It would also support the verification and monitoring processes by linking financial flows to defined ecological outcomes. Regulatory authorities and standard-setting bodies can support this by developing and endorsing classification frameworks that are science-based, aligned with global climate and biodiversity goals, and adaptable to national contexts.

Establishing clear regulatory standards enhances the legitimacy and impact of blue bonds while facilitating comparability across issuances. This, in turn, strengthens the integrity of the market and supports the scale-up of investment in ocean sustainability.

1.3 Legal and Institutional Architecture

A robust legal and institutional architecture is central to the effective design, issuance, and management of blue bonds. Legal frameworks provide the necessary authority for governments, municipalities, or corporations to issue debt instruments, while institutional arrangements ensure oversight, coordination, and implementation. Together, these elements create a predictable and secure environment that supports investor confidence and the successful execution of ocean-related projects.

The legal foundation for issuing blue bonds typically builds upon existing legislation governing sovereign or municipal debt, securities, and public finance. In many jurisdictions, enabling laws may need to be amended or clarified to allow for thematic bonds with environmental objectives. This includes defining eligible expenditures, compliance requirements, and the allocation of responsibilities among public institutions. Legal provisions may also establish requirements for transparency, disclosure, and independent verification to safeguard the integrity of the instrument.

Institutionally, effective governance requires coordination across multiple ministries and agencies, including finance, environment, fisheries, infrastructure, and planning. Establishing inter-agency task forces or dedicated blue finance units can improve project selection, streamline decision-making, and ensure alignment with national development goals. These entities can also serve as focal points for stakeholder engagement, capacity building, and international collaboration.

Furthermore, the involvement of independent oversight bodies, such as public auditors or environmental regulators, can strengthen accountability in the use of proceeds. Legal contracts and covenants should clearly articulate the obligations of issuers and implementers, including performance benchmarks and consequences for non-compliance.

By embedding blue bonds within sound legal frameworks and supported by capable institutions, countries and organizations can establish the conditions necessary for transparent, accountable, and effective use of finance in support of ocean sustainability. This legal and institutional clarity is essential for scaling up investment and attracting long-term capital to the blue economy.

1.4 Monitoring, Reporting, and Verification (MRV) Requirements

Effective MRV systems are essential to ensure transparency, accountability, and credibility in the blue bond market. These systems provide a structured approach for tracking how bond proceeds are allocated, measuring environmental and social impacts, and validating performance against stated objectives. A robust MRV framework supports investor confidence, reduces the risk of green or bluewashing, and enhances the overall integrity of blue finance instruments.

Monitoring involves the systematic collection of data on project implementation and financial disbursements. Issuers must establish internal processes to track the flow of proceeds and ensure alignment with predefined eligible activities, such as marine habitat restoration, pollution prevention, or sustainable coastal infrastructure. Monitoring mechanisms should be embedded in project design from the outset and linked to measurable indicators that reflect environmental and social outcomes.

Reporting translates monitoring results into structured disclosures made available to investors and stakeholders. These reports typically include details on the use of proceeds, project progress, key performance indicators, and any deviations from planned implementation. Regular reporting—annually or semi-annually—is a common practice and should follow standardized formats to enable comparability across issuers and projects.

Verification is the independent review of both the use of proceeds and the achievement of impact outcomes. This may be conducted by accredited third-party verifiers who assess whether the project aligns with stated blue bond criteria and whether reported data is accurate and reliable. Verification can occur at multiple stages, including pre-issuance validation, ongoing assurance, and post-implementation evaluation.

Governments and regulators can enhance MRV quality by requiring issuers to adopt internationally recognized reporting standards, such as those developed by ICMA or the Climate Bonds Initiative. Encouraging third-party assurance and public disclosure further strengthens transparency. As the blue bond market grows, consistent and credible MRV practices will be key to ensuring that financing contributes meaningfully to ocean sustainability and builds long-term trust with investors.

1.5 Enhancing Policy Coherence and Risk Reduction

Policy coherence and risk reduction are critical to the success and scalability of blue bonds. Given the cross-sectoral nature of marine and coastal sustainability, effective coordination between policies related to finance, environment, fisheries, climate, and infrastructure is necessary to avoid duplication, reduce inefficiencies, and improve the effectiveness of blue bond initiatives. A coherent policy environment ensures that blue bonds are aligned with national priorities and international commitments, reinforcing their legitimacy and appeal to investors.

Policy coherence begins with integrated planning. Governments can align blue bond strategies with marine spatial plans, climate adaptation frameworks, and biodiversity targets to ensure that financed projects support broader national development goals. Establishing formal coordination mechanisms between ministries and agencies can improve project selection, streamline implementation, and enhance oversight. This integrated approach reduces the likelihood of conflicting regulations or fragmented responsibilities that can deter investment and delay execution.

In parallel, reducing financial risk is essential to attract private capital into the blue bond market, particularly in countries with limited fiscal space or weaker institutional capacity. Risk reduction mechanisms such as sovereign guarantees, partial credit risk guarantees, and political risk insurance can improve the creditworthiness of issuers and enhance investor confidence.

Development finance institutions and multilateral banks can play a catalytic role by providing these instruments or co-investing in blue bond transactions.

Public-private dialogue is also important in identifying and addressing investment barriers. Engaging financial institutions, insurers, and technical experts early in the policy design process helps ensure that regulatory frameworks are practical and responsive to market needs. Incentives such as tax benefits, regulatory recognition, or preferential treatment under investment guidelines can further enhance the attractiveness of blue bonds.

By fostering policy coherence and implementing targeted risk mitigation strategies, governments and stakeholders can create a stable enabling environment for blue bonds. This not only facilitates the flow of capital toward sustainable ocean activities but also contributes to broader economic resilience and climate goals.

Chapter 2: Financing Structures and Market Development Strategies

Scaling the blue bond market requires fit-for-purpose financing structures and supportive market development strategies. As interest in ocean-focused investment grows, the challenge lies in designing bond instruments that are financially sound, environmentally credible, and accessible to a range of issuers—from sovereigns and municipalities to corporations and development banks.

Effective blue bond structures must align investor expectations with sustainability outcomes while addressing risk, liquidity, and regulatory considerations. Equally important is the creation of a robust pipeline of investable projects and the removal of structural barriers that limit market entry, particularly in emerging economies.

This chapter examines the financial mechanics and ecosystem required to grow the blue bond market. It covers bond typologies, blended finance approaches, investor engagement, pipeline development, and strategies to overcome key market constraints. Together, these elements form a practical framework for mobilizing capital at scale to support sustainable ocean economies.

2.1 Blue Bond Typologies and Financial Structures

Blue bonds can be structured in various forms depending on the issuer, the intended use of proceeds, and the performance expectations associated with the investment. Understanding the different typologies and financial structures is essential for designing instruments that meet the needs of both issuers and investors, while maintaining credibility and alignment with sustainability objectives.

The most common type is the use-of-proceeds blue bond, where capital raised is allocated specifically to eligible ocean-related projects. These bonds are typically aligned with established frameworks such as the Green Bond Principles, with the distinction that proceeds are directed exclusively to marine and coastal initiatives. Issuers commit to financing or refinancing projects such as marine conservation, wastewater treatment, coastal infrastructure, or sustainable fisheries, and are expected to report on how funds are used and the impacts achieved.

A second category includes sustainability-linked blue bonds, which tie financial or structural features of the bond—such as coupon rates—to the achievement of predefined key performance indicators (KPIs) related to ocean sustainability. These bonds offer issuers greater flexibility in how proceeds are used but require strong monitoring and verification systems to track progress toward stated goals.

In terms of issuer types, blue bonds may be issued by sovereign governments, subnational entities, state-owned enterprises, development banks, or private corporations. The structure may vary accordingly. For example, sovereign issuances may benefit from higher credit ratings and broader market access, while corporate issuances often require detailed disclosures and third-party verification to meet investor expectations.

Credit enhancements, guarantees, and blended finance structures can be integrated to improve the risk-return profile of blue bonds, particularly in emerging markets. Ultimately, the chosen structure should align with the issuer's financial strategy, institutional capacity, and the environmental outcomes being targeted, ensuring the bond's credibility and effectiveness in mobilizing capital for ocean sustainability.

2.2 Blended Finance and De-Risking Mechanisms

Blended finance and de-risking mechanisms are essential tools for scaling up investment in blue bonds, particularly in emerging and developing economies where perceived financial and political risks may deter private sector participation. By strategically combining public, philanthropic, and concessional capital with private investment, blended finance structures can improve the risk-return profile of blue bond transactions and catalyze capital flows into ocean sustainability.

Blended finance approaches often involve the use of concessional funding from development finance institutions (DFIs), multilateral development banks (MDBs), or donor agencies to absorb initial risk, offer first-loss capital, or provide subordinated debt. This layered approach enables commercial investors to enter blue bond markets with greater confidence, knowing that some of the downside risk is mitigated. Additionally, grant-based technical assistance can support project preparation, capacity building, and impact assessment, improving overall bankability.

De-risking instruments such as credit guarantees, political risk insurance, and foreign exchange hedging can further enhance investor confidence. Credit guarantees can partially or fully cover bond repayment in the event of default, while political risk insurance protects against non-commercial risks such as expropriation, currency inconvertibility, or regulatory changes. These tools are particularly relevant for sovereign and subnational issuers in countries with limited credit histories or weaker institutional frameworks.

Public finance institutions play a catalytic role in structuring and deploying these tools. By aligning incentives and absorbing targeted risks, they help bridge financing gaps and encourage private capital to invest in projects that contribute to marine and coastal resilience. A well-designed blended finance approach ensures that public and concessional resources are used strategically to unlock larger volumes of private investment, while maintaining a focus on environmental integrity and social impact. This approach is central to the long-term success and scalability of the blue bond market.

2.3 Investor Landscape and Incentive Alignment

The investor landscape for blue bonds is diverse and evolving, encompassing institutional investors, development banks, sovereign wealth funds, private asset managers, and impact-focused investors. Each category brings different risk appetites, return expectations, and sustainability mandates, making it essential to align incentives and tailor offerings to suit their investment criteria while maintaining the environmental integrity of blue bonds.

Institutional investors—such as pension funds, insurance companies, and mutual funds—seek predictable returns and compliance with fiduciary duties. For these investors, blue bonds must offer creditworthy structures, transparent reporting, and alignment with environmental, social, and governance (ESG) frameworks. Clear linkage to recognized taxonomies and performance benchmarks can help address concerns about risk and credibility.

Impact investors and philanthropic capital providers may place greater emphasis on social and environmental outcomes. These stakeholders are more likely to accept below-market returns or higher risks if impact is measurable and verified. Aligning with their goals requires robust monitoring systems and impact indicators that clearly demonstrate the contribution of blue bond projects to ocean sustainability.

Development banks and multilateral institutions can serve dual roles as both investors and risk mitigators. Their participation in blue bond transactions provides market validation and can signal credibility to other investors. Additionally, they can offer technical assistance and support the development of enabling regulatory environments.

To attract and retain investor interest, issuers must provide clear disclosures, consistent performance updates, and reliable impact data. Incorporating incentives such as performance-linked pricing or preferred regulatory treatment can further enhance attractiveness. Engagement between issuers and investors during the structuring phase helps ensure that blue bonds meet market expectations without compromising on sustainability objectives. Ultimately, aligning investor incentives with environmental impact is critical to expanding the pool of capital available for ocean-related projects and building a resilient blue finance market.

2.4 Market Development and Pipeline Creation

The long-term viability of the blue bond market depends on the development of a consistent pipeline of investable projects and the establishment of supporting market infrastructure. Many countries, particularly in the Global South, face challenges in identifying, preparing, and scaling projects that are suitable for bond financing. Addressing these gaps requires coordinated efforts across public institutions, development partners, and private sector stakeholders.

Developing a blue project pipeline begins with identifying priority areas aligned with national ocean policies, climate strategies, and sustainable development goals. These may include sustainable fisheries, marine biodiversity protection, wastewater treatment, and coastal infrastructure. Governments and public agencies can support this process by mapping existing initiatives, assessing financing needs, and screening projects for technical and financial viability.

Capacity building is essential to help potential issuers—such as governments, municipalities, and state-owned enterprises— understand blue bond issuance processes, disclosure requirements, and investor expectations. Technical assistance can also support the preparation of feasibility studies, environmental assessments, and impact frameworks, ensuring that projects meet eligibility criteria and are attractive to investors.

Market development is further strengthened by partnerships with financial institutions, underwriters, and advisory firms that bring expertise in bond structuring and placement. Engaging with verification agencies and rating providers at an early stage can facilitate transparent and credible issuance. In parallel, governments and multilateral organizations can develop centralized blue finance platforms to promote pipeline visibility and attract investor interest.

Establishing a steady flow of credible, well-prepared projects helps to deepen the blue bond market and create opportunities for repeat issuances. Over time, a mature project pipeline, supported by institutional readiness and investor confidence, enables the market to scale and contributes to sustained financing for ocean sustainability objectives.

2.5 Overcoming Barriers to Scale

Despite growing interest in blue bonds, several barriers continue to limit their scale and accessibility. Addressing these challenges is essential for expanding the market, attracting a broader range of investors, and ensuring that capital is directed toward impactful and sustainable ocean-related projects.

One significant barrier is the limited availability of bankable projects. Many potential initiatives in the marine and coastal space lack the technical preparation, financial structuring, or data needed to meet investor requirements. This is particularly pronounced in developing countries, where capacity constraints and fragmented project ownership hinder the development of viable investment opportunities.

High transaction costs also pose a challenge, especially for smaller issuances. The need for external certification, impact assessments, legal reviews, and investor outreach can be resource-intensive and time-consuming. Pooling smaller projects into thematic portfolios or using aggregation platforms may help lower costs and achieve economies of scale.

Market fragmentation and the absence of standardized frameworks make it difficult for investors to compare blue bond offerings across regions and issuers. Without harmonized definitions, taxonomies, and reporting formats, there is a risk of inconsistency and reduced market credibility. Global coordination and the development of universally accepted guidelines can help establish clarity and comparability.

In addition, a lack of data—particularly reliable, science-based marine and environmental data—limits effective monitoring and impact measurement. Investment in ocean data infrastructure and disclosure systems is needed to support transparency and build trust.

Overcoming these barriers requires a combination of targeted policy interventions, technical support, and financial innovation. Strengthening institutional capacity, standardizing processes, and enhancing public-private collaboration can create a more enabling environment. By addressing these systemic issues, stakeholders can unlock the full potential of blue bonds as a scalable financing mechanism for ocean sustainability.

Chapter 3: Technology, Data, and Impact Measurement Systems

Technology and data systems play a critical role in ensuring transparency, accountability, and effectiveness in the blue bond market. As financial flows toward ocean sustainability increase, so too does the need for tools that can monitor project performance, verify environmental outcomes, and safeguard digital integrity.

Emerging technologies such as blockchain, remote sensing, and AI offer opportunities to enhance tracking and reporting, reduce manual oversight, and support real-time decision-making. At the same time, the availability and quality of ocean data remain uneven, particularly in regions most vulnerable to climate and marine pressures.

This chapter explores how digital tools and data infrastructure can strengthen the credibility and functionality of blue bonds. It covers investment transparency systems, ocean monitoring technologies, disclosure platforms, predictive analytics, and cybersecurity measures—each contributing to a more robust, efficient, and trustworthy blue finance ecosystem.

3.1 Digital Tools for Ocean Investment Transparency

Digital tools are playing an increasingly important role in enhancing transparency and accountability within the blue bond market. These technologies can improve the tracking of financial flows, ensure adherence to environmental commitments, and support data-driven decision-making. As investors seek greater visibility into how funds are allocated and what outcomes are achieved, digital solutions offer scalable mechanisms for real-time monitoring and reporting.

Blockchain technology, for example, enables transparent and tamper-proof tracking of how bond proceeds are used. By creating an immutable ledger, blockchain systems can record each transaction from bond issuance to project implementation, allowing stakeholders to verify whether funds are being directed toward eligible activities. This traceability helps reduce the risk of misallocation and strengthens trust between issuers and investors.

Smart contracts—self-executing agreements coded into blockchain platforms—can automate disbursement of funds based on pre-agreed conditions. For instance, funds may only be released once specific milestones are verified, such as the completion of a marine restoration activity or installation of pollution control systems. These mechanisms can improve efficiency and reduce administrative overhead.

Digital dashboards and investor portals can provide real-time access to key performance indicators, project updates, and impact metrics. These platforms enhance engagement by enabling investors to monitor progress, assess risk, and understand the contribution of their investments to sustainability outcomes. They also support greater public transparency when made accessible to broader stakeholders.

The integration of digital tools must be accompanied by appropriate governance structures to ensure data accuracy, system interoperability, and cybersecurity. When designed and implemented effectively, these technologies contribute to more reliable, transparent, and verifiable blue bond transactions. In doing so, they support market credibility and help scale the adoption of blue finance by addressing core concerns around monitoring, reporting, and impact verification.

3.2 Ocean Data Infrastructure and Monitoring Systems

Reliable ocean data infrastructure and monitoring systems are fundamental to the effectiveness of blue bonds. These systems provide the empirical foundation needed to assess project eligibility, track implementation, and measure environmental outcomes. As investment in marine and coastal sustainability increases, the ability to collect, analyze, and share high-quality data becomes essential for ensuring that projects are evidence-based and aligned with intended objectives.

Modern ocean monitoring systems combine technologies such as satellite-based Earth observation, autonomous underwater vehicles, remote sensing, and IoT-enabled sensors deployed on buoys and coastal infrastructure. These tools can provide real-time data on ocean temperature, salinity, water quality, biodiversity indicators, and other critical parameters. When integrated into monitoring frameworks, they support timely decision-making and adaptive management of blue bond-funded projects.

In addition to technology deployment, institutional capacity to manage and interpret data is critical. National oceanographic institutes, environmental agencies, and research organizations play key roles in maintaining data platforms, developing indicators, and validating findings. Building technical capacity and investing in data infrastructure can help ensure long-term monitoring and strengthen project credibility.

Open-access ocean data portals and global initiatives, such as the UN Decade of Ocean Science and the Global Ocean Observing System (GOOS), contribute to data standardization and transparency. These platforms allow for wider access to ocean data, supporting independent analysis, cross-border collaboration, and policy alignment.

Challenges remain around data gaps, especially in developing countries with limited technical resources or sparse monitoring networks. Addressing these gaps requires targeted investment, international cooperation, and integration of traditional and community-based knowledge systems.

A well-developed ocean data infrastructure underpins the monitoring and verification systems required for blue bonds. By supporting transparency, enabling impact assessment, and strengthening investor confidence, it forms a critical component of a functioning and credible blue finance ecosystem.

3.3 Platforms for Blue Bond Tracking and Disclosure

Dedicated platforms for tracking and disclosure are increasingly necessary to support the transparency and accountability of blue bond markets. These platforms serve as central repositories for financial, operational, and environmental data, enabling stakeholders to access consistent information on the issuance, implementation, and impact of blue bond-financed projects. As the market grows, the development of standardized and accessible tracking systems becomes essential for ensuring comparability, reducing information asymmetries, and building trust among investors, regulators, and the public.

A well-functioning disclosure platform typically includes data on the bond issuer, use of proceeds, project locations, implementation status, and relevant performance indicators. For investors, this information helps evaluate alignment with environmental, social, and governance (ESG) criteria and assess whether the investment meets risk and return expectations. For regulators and certifiers, it facilitates oversight and verification against eligibility criteria and impact benchmarks.

Digital platforms can be designed to integrate with existing sustainability reporting frameworks, such as those developed by the ICMA, the Task Force on Climate-related Financial Disclosures (TCFD), and the Global Reporting Initiative (GRI). Compatibility with these frameworks supports harmonization and reduces the reporting burden on issuers while ensuring that disclosures meet global standards.

Interactive dashboards and visual reporting tools enhance user engagement by allowing real-time access to project data and progress updates. Some platforms may also include geospatial data and mapping features to display the geographic scope of blue bond investments and their relation to marine ecosystems or coastal zones.

Public access to these platforms contributes to market transparency and stakeholder accountability. At the same time, secure access controls and data governance protocols are needed to protect sensitive information. As blue finance instruments expand, centralized and standardized tracking and disclosure systems will play a central role in sustaining market integrity and investor confidence.

3.4 AI and Predictive Analytics in Blue Finance

Artificial intelligence (AI) and predictive analytics are becoming valuable tools in the development and management of blue finance, offering enhanced capabilities for forecasting, risk assessment, and decision-making. These technologies can analyze large and complex datasets, identify patterns and trends, and generate insights that support evidence-based planning and performance monitoring in blue bond-funded projects.

In the context of ocean sustainability, AI can process data from multiple sources—such as satellite imagery, remote sensors, and environmental databases—to monitor changes in marine ecosystems, detect anomalies, and assess project impacts. Predictive models can estimate the likely outcomes of interventions, such as coral reef restoration or coastal infrastructure upgrades, under different environmental and climate scenarios. These insights support adaptive project design and improve the likelihood of achieving long-term ecological and financial goals.

AI-driven tools can also assist in financial risk analysis by simulating market conditions, modeling default probabilities, and stress-testing project performance under various environmental shocks. This helps issuers and investors identify vulnerabilities, plan mitigation strategies, and make informed decisions about investment structure and timing.

For impact measurement, AI enables the automation of data collection and classification, reducing the manual effort involved in monitoring and reporting. Natural language processing and image recognition technologies can enhance the efficiency and consistency of qualitative and visual assessments, particularly in remote or data-scarce regions.

While the use of AI in blue finance is still emerging, it offers significant potential to enhance transparency, reduce uncertainty, and optimize project performance. However, careful attention must be given to data quality, algorithmic bias, and the interpretability of models. Integrating AI tools with established governance and disclosure frameworks ensures that technology complements rather than replaces human oversight. As digital capabilities expand, AI and predictive analytics are expected to play an increasingly important role in scaling and securing the future of blue finance.

3.5 Cybersecurity and Digital Integrity

As digital tools become more integrated into the governance and management of blue bonds, ensuring cybersecurity and digital integrity is critical. The increasing reliance on data platforms, blockchain technologies, smart contracts, and cloud-based reporting systems exposes blue finance infrastructure to potential vulnerabilities. Protecting sensitive financial data, project performance metrics, and stakeholder information is essential to maintain trust, uphold transparency, and prevent disruptions that could undermine the credibility of the market.

Cybersecurity refers to the protection of digital systems from unauthorized access, data breaches, and cyberattacks. For blue bond issuers and administrators, this includes securing investor portals, digital ledgers, and databases that house financial and environmental data. Strong authentication protocols, encryption standards, and regular security audits are necessary to safeguard these systems from both internal and external threats.

Digital integrity involves maintaining the accuracy, consistency, and authenticity of data throughout its lifecycle. This is especially important in a market that depends on accurate reporting of environmental outcomes and responsible use of proceeds. Systems must ensure that data inputs cannot be manipulated and that reporting outputs reflect verified performance. Incorporating blockchain can support this by creating immutable transaction records, but even these systems require oversight and maintenance.

Cross-border coordination presents additional cybersecurity challenges. Many blue bond initiatives involve international investors, multilaterals, and technical partners, requiring consistent standards for data protection and privacy compliance. Harmonizing cybersecurity practices across jurisdictions can help reduce fragmentation and improve resilience.

Investments in cybersecurity capacity—through personnel training, digital infrastructure upgrades, and partnerships with security firms—should be part of broader efforts to digitize and scale blue finance. By prioritizing cybersecurity and digital integrity, stakeholders can ensure that the digital foundations of the blue bond ecosystem remain secure, reliable, and resilient in the face of evolving technological and environmental risks.

Conclusion

Blue bonds represent a strategic opportunity to mobilize finance for the sustainable development of marine and coastal ecosystems. As the world seeks to address the interconnected challenges of climate change, biodiversity loss, and ocean degradation, blue bonds offer a targeted financial instrument capable of channeling investment into critical areas such as marine conservation, pollution control, and coastal resilience. Their growing relevance reflects the broader recognition of the ocean's role in supporting global environmental and economic stability.

Realizing the full potential of blue bonds requires coordinated action across three core dimensions: enabling policy frameworks, innovative financial structures, and reliable digital systems. Strong public policy and governance are necessary to define standards, ensure oversight, and align blue finance with national and international priorities. Financial innovation and risk mitigation tools can attract a wider range of investors, while technological advancements in monitoring and data infrastructure support transparency and accountability.

Global decision-makers—across governments, development institutions, and the private sector—have a key role to play in advancing the blue bond market. By supporting regulatory clarity, project readiness, and digital integrity, stakeholders can create the conditions necessary for scaling adoption. Strengthening these foundations will enable blue bonds to become a core component of sustainable finance and a driver of long-term ocean resilience.

www.ingramcontent.com/pod-product-compliance
Lightning Source LLC
Chambersburg PA
CBHW060532280326
41933CB00014B/3144